BIOGR

KAWHI LEONARD

one of the greatest two-way players in NBA history

Jack K. Rowell

Copyright © 2025 – All rights reserved

All rights reserved. No part of this book may be reproduced in any form or by any electronic or mechanical means, including information storage and retrieval systems, without permission in writing from the publisher, except by a reviewer, who may quote brief passages in a review.

Legal Notice:

This book is copyright-protected. It is only for personal use, you cannot amend, distribute, sell, use, quote, or paraphrase any part, or the content within this book either directly or indirectly.

TABLE OF CONTENT

INTRODUCTION 4
CHAPTER 1: EARLY LIFE 8
CHAPTER 2: HIGH SCHOOL CAREER 13
CHAPTER 3: COLLEGE YEARS 18
CHAPTER 4: ENTRY INTO THE NBA 26
CHAPTER 5: RISE TO STARDOM 33
CHAPTER 6: THE TORONTO RAPTORS ERA 40
CHAPTER 7: LA CLIPPERS JOURNEY 48
CHAPTER 8: PERSONALITY AND OFF-COURT LIFE 55
CHAPTER 9: LEGACY AND IMPACT 61
CONCLUSION 68

INTRODUCTION

Kawhi Leonard's name is synonymous with excellence in basketball, but his significance extends far beyond his impressive statistics and accolades. Leonard represents the epitome of perseverance and humility in a sport often dominated by larger-than-life personalities and constant media scrutiny. His journey, characterized by relentless effort, laser-sharp focus, and resilience born from personal loss and professional challenges, has made him a role model for aspiring athletes and fans worldwide.

Few players in NBA history have managed to achieve what Kawhi Leonard has accomplished in such a short period. As a two-time NBA champion and Finals MVP, his legacy is already cemented. Yet, what sets him apart isn't just his success but the unique way he achieves it. Leonard operates in a manner that defies conventional expectations. While others chase headlines, he quietly delivers, letting his performance on the court speak volumes. His introverted nature and measured responses to the media have added an air of mystery to his persona, making him one of the most intriguing figures in modern sports.

This biography aims to delve deep into Leonard's life, from his humble beginnings in Riverside, California, to his rise as one of the most dominant forces in professional basketball. It will explore the pivotal moments that defined his career, including his emergence as a defensive specialist with the San Antonio Spurs, his unforgettable championship run with the

Toronto Raptors, and his ongoing quest for greatness with the Los Angeles Clippers. Along the way, we will uncover the challenges he faced, including devastating personal losses, injuries, and the immense pressure of being an NBA superstar.

But this book is about more than just basketball. Kawhi Leonard's story is one of character and conviction. It's about a man who remained true to himself in a world that often demands conformity. His commitment to family, his unrelenting work ethic, and his quiet but impactful presence off the court reveal the depth of his character.

The objective of this biography is twofold: first, to provide an intimate portrait of Kawhi Leonard as a person and athlete, and second, to examine the broader impact he has had on the game of basketball and beyond. In understanding Kawhi, we gain insight into what it takes to achieve greatness, not through flash and spectacle, but through discipline, focus, and sheer determination. This is the story of Kawhi Leonard—a man of few words but countless achievements.

CHAPTER 1: EARLY LIFE

Kawhi Anthony Leonard was born on June 29, 1991, in Los Angeles, California, and raised in nearby Riverside. From the beginning, Kawhi's life was deeply rooted in family and community. The youngest of five siblings, he grew up surrounded by strong familial bonds that would later become a cornerstone of his identity. His parents, Mark Leonard and Kim Robertson played critical roles in shaping his character, instilling values of hard work, humility, and resilience.

Family Background and Riverside Upbringing

Riverside, a city known for its rich diversity and tight-knit neighborhoods, was where Kawhi spent his formative years. His upbringing was modest but filled with love and support. Mark Leonard, Kawhi's father, was a hardworking man who owned a car wash. He taught Kawhi the value of perseverance and determination by example, working long hours to provide for the family.

Kawhi's mother, Kim, was equally influential, nurturing her children and encouraging them to pursue their passions. Despite their parents' separation when Kawhi was young, both remained actively involved in his life. His older sisters often took on protective roles, helping to keep him grounded and focused.

The streets of Riverside, though vibrant, were not without challenges. Kawhi grew up in an environment where distractions and temptations were plentiful, but his family's emphasis on discipline and responsibility helped him stay on the right path. He would later credit his upbringing for the mental toughness that became a hallmark of his basketball career.

Childhood Interests and Athletic Talent

As a child, Kawhi exhibited a quiet demeanor, a trait that would follow him throughout his life. But when it came to sports, he came alive. Initially, he showed a love for football, playing the game passionately during his elementary and middle school years. As a wide receiver, Kawhi's speed and agility were undeniable, and some believed he had the potential for a future in the sport.

However, basketball soon emerged as his true calling. Kawhi spent countless hours on the court, often shooting hoops late into the night. His passion for the game was matched by his natural talent. Even as a young boy, he displayed an uncanny ability to read plays, a relentless work ethic, and a calm composure under pressure. His dedication to improving his skills was apparent to anyone who watched him play.

The Role of His Father, Mark Leonard

Mark Leonard was more than just a father to Kawhi—he was his biggest supporter and motivator. Mark frequently took Kawhi to his car wash, where the young boy would help out between school and basketball practice. These moments were not just about work but about life lessons. Mark emphasized the importance of earning success through effort and staying humble regardless of achievements.

Mark was also instrumental in Kawhi's basketball development, often attending his games and offering constructive feedback. He was a constant presence, encouraging Kawhi to push himself and never settle for mediocrity. Tragically, this relationship was cut short when Mark Leonard was fatally shot at his car wash in

2008—a loss that devastated Kawhi and forever changed his life.

Despite the heartbreak, Kawhi channeled his grief into his passion for basketball. The memory of his father became a driving force, motivating him to honor Mark's legacy through his accomplishments on the court. This profound loss marked a turning point in Kawhi's life, solidifying the quiet resilience and determination for which he would later become known.

Kawhi Leonard's early years laid the foundation for the player and person he would become. His family's influence, combined with the challenges he faced, forged a character defined by strength, humility, and an unyielding drive to succeed. Even as a child, the seeds of greatness were evident—a testament to the powerful role his upbringing played in shaping his future.

CHAPTER 2: HIGH SCHOOL CAREER

Kawhi Leonard's high school basketball career was the crucible in which his legendary work ethic and understated leadership began to take shape. His journey through Canyon Springs High School and Martin Luther King High School revealed a player of immense potential, raw talent, and an unrelenting drive to improve.

The Beginning at Canyon Springs High School

Kawhi began his high school career at Canyon Springs High School in Moreno Valley, California. Although his talent was evident, he was still a lanky teenager trying to find his place in the sport. At Canyon Springs, Kawhi started to stand out for his defensive skills and rebounding ability, traits that would later define his NBA career. Even at a young age, he demonstrated a deep understanding of the game, often outsmarting more physically mature opponents with his basketball IQ.

However, circumstances shifted when Kawhi transferred to Martin Luther King High School in Riverside for his junior year. The move was driven by his family's desire to give him a better environment to develop both academically and athletically. At King High, Kawhi found the stability and support he needed to elevate his game.

Dominance at Martin Luther King High School

At Martin Luther King High School, Kawhi began to transform from a promising player into a dominant force. His junior year saw him emerge as a standout performer, averaging impressive numbers and leading his team in crucial moments. By his senior year, Kawhi was a star, averaging 22.6 points, 13.1 rebounds, 3.9 assists, and 3.0 blocks per game. He helped lead the Wolves to a stellar season and gained recognition as one of the best high school players in California.

Despite his growing reputation, Kawhi remained grounded. His coaches often marveled at his quiet demeanor and ability to lead by example. Unlike many players of his caliber, he didn't seek attention or accolades. Instead, he let his work on the court do the talking.

Key Achievements, Challenges, and Growth

One of Kawhi's defining traits during his high school years was his resilience. He faced a significant setback when he and his team fell short in a crucial playoff game, but rather than dwelling on the loss, Kawhi used it as motivation to work harder. That offseason, he transformed his body and refined his skills, setting the stage for an exceptional senior year.

Among his many accolades, Kawhi was named California Mr. Basketball in 2009, an honor that cemented his status as one of the top high school players in the state. Despite these achievements, he remained a relatively underrated prospect on the national stage. This lack of widespread recognition would become a recurring theme in his career and one of his greatest motivators.

Work Ethic and Quiet Demeanor

Even as a teenager, Kawhi's work ethic was extraordinary. He was known to arrive at the gym hours before practice to work on his shot and stay long after his teammates had left. His coaches often recalled how he would spend hours perfecting the fundamentals, from free throws to defensive drills, demonstrating a level of focus and commitment far beyond his years.

Kawhi's quiet demeanor also began to crystallize during these years. He wasn't the vocal leader who would rally his teammates with fiery speeches. Instead, he led by example, pushing himself to the limit and inspiring those around him to do the same. His reserved nature earned him respect from his peers, who admired his unwavering determination and focus on the game.

Kawhi Leonard's high school career laid the groundwork for the player he would become. Through hard work, perseverance, and an unwavering commitment to excellence, he turned raw talent into refined skill. His time at Canyon Springs and Martin Luther King High School was a testament to his resilience and quiet determination—a foreshadowing of the greatness that was yet to come.

CHAPTER 3: COLLEGE YEARS

Kawhi Leonard's college career at San Diego State University (SDSU) was the stage where raw talent met an unrelenting drive to improve. Over two seasons, he blossomed into a player who could dominate on both ends of the court while remaining grounded and focused. This chapter explores how his time at SDSU shaped his game, propelled the Aztecs basketball program to new heights, and laid the foundation for his rise to NBA stardom.

Recruitment Journey and Decision to Attend SDSU

Kawhi's recruitment story was a testament to his underrated potential. Despite a stellar high school career, he was not heavily pursued by blue-chip college programs like Duke or Kentucky. His relatively low national ranking, combined with his quiet demeanor, meant he flew under the radar of most major recruiters. However, Steve Fisher, the head coach at SDSU, saw something special in Kawhi—a rare combination of raw athleticism, versatility, and an insatiable hunger to improve.

Kawhi's decision to attend SDSU was influenced by a few key factors. Staying close to home allowed him to maintain the support system of his family, which was crucial after the loss of his father. SDSU also offered an opportunity to play immediately, rather than waiting behind upperclassmen as might have been the case at larger programs. Most importantly, Coach Fisher and his staff promised to help Kawhi reach his full potential, both as a player and as a person.

While the Aztecs were not yet considered a powerhouse program, they were on the rise, and Kawhi's arrival coincided with a turning point for the team. His commitment to SDSU signaled his confidence in the program and his willingness to be a key figure in building something special.

Successes with the Aztecs Basketball Team

From his first game as a freshman in the 2009-2010 season, Kawhi Leonard made his presence known. Standing at 6'7" with a 7'3" wingspan, he was a matchup nightmare for opponents. His defensive instincts, rebounding ability, and physicality made an immediate impact. Kawhi's ability to crash the boards, even against bigger players, earned him praise from teammates and opponents alike.

As a freshman, Kawhi averaged 12.7 points and 9.9 rebounds per game, a double-double that underscored his value to the team. He was a driving force behind SDSU's success that season, helping the Aztecs win the Mountain West Conference (MWC) tournament and earn a spot in the NCAA Tournament. Though they exited in the first round, Kawhi's performances showcased his potential to carry a team on the national stage.

His sophomore season in 2010-2011 was a revelation. Kawhi improved in every aspect of his game, averaging 15.7 points and 10.4 rebounds per game while adding more offensive versatility to his repertoire. His shooting range expanded, and his ability to create scoring opportunities for himself and his teammates grew significantly. Kawhi led the Aztecs to a program-best 34-3 record, earning them national attention and a ranking in the top 10 for much of the season.

Mountain West Conference Titles

Winning the Mountain West Conference championship became a hallmark of Kawhi's time at SDSU. Under his leadership, the Aztecs captured back-to-back MWC titles in 2010 and 2011. These victories not only showcased the team's dominance within their conference but also highlighted Kawhi's ability to rise to the occasion in crucial games.

His performances in the conference tournaments were particularly noteworthy. Whether it was pulling down rebounds in traffic, hitting clutch shots, or locking down the opposing team's best player, Kawhi proved time and again that he could be counted on when it mattered most.

NCAA Tournament Appearances

Kawhi's sophomore year culminated in an impressive run in the NCAA Tournament. As a No. 2 seed, the Aztecs cruised through the early rounds, reaching the Sweet 16 for the first time in program history. In those high-stakes games, Kawhi delivered some of his most memorable performances, averaging double-doubles and showcasing his trademark calm under pressure.

Although the Aztecs' season ended with a hard-fought loss to the eventual national champion, the University of Connecticut, the tournament solidified Kawhi's status as one of college basketball's brightest stars. Scouts took notice of his ability to perform on the biggest stages, and analysts praised his leadership and versatility.

Developing His Game and Gaining National Attention

Kawhi's time at SDSU was marked by relentless self-improvement. His commitment to mastering the fundamentals set him apart from his peers. Whether it was refining his jump shot, working on his ball-handling, or studying film to better understand defensive rotations, Kawhi's work ethic became legendary. He was known to spend hours in the gym, often long after his teammates had left, honing every aspect of his game.

Off the court, Kawhi remained true to his reserved nature. He wasn't the loud, charismatic figure that many star athletes were, but his quiet confidence and consistent excellence earned him the respect of coaches, teammates, and opponents alike.

By the end of his sophomore year, Kawhi Leonard had become a Consensus Second-Team All-American and one of the most coveted players in college basketball. His decision to declare for the NBA Draft was met with widespread approval, as it was clear he had the skills, mindset, and physical tools to succeed at the next level.

Kawhi Leonard's college career was a microcosm of what would define him as a professional—unwavering focus, relentless effort, and a knack for excelling under pressure. His time at SDSU not only elevated the program to national prominence but also established Kawhi as a rising star, ready to take the next step on his journey to greatness.

CHAPTER 4: ENTRY INTO THE NBA

Kawhi Leonard's entry into the NBA was a pivotal chapter in his life, filled with challenges, growth, and the kind of transformation that would set the stage for a storied career. From being drafted by the Indiana Pacers and traded to the San Antonio Spurs to evolving from a raw rookie to one of the league's premier defensive players, Kawhi's early years in the NBA were a testament to his adaptability, perseverance, and willingness to learn from some of the game's greatest minds.

Drafting by the Indiana Pacers and traded to the San Antonio Spurs

The 2011 NBA Draft was a night of mixed emotions for Kawhi Leonard. Despite an impressive college career at San Diego State, many scouts questioned whether his game would translate to the professional level. Concerns about his shooting mechanics and his offensive skill set caused him to slide down draft boards. Ultimately, he was selected as the 15th overall pick by the Indiana Pacers.

However, Kawhi's time as a Pacer lasted only a few moments. In a draft-night trade, the Pacers sent him to the San Antonio Spurs in exchange for point guard George Hill, a move that would alter the trajectory of both Kawhi's career and the Spurs' legacy. For the Spurs, the trade was a calculated risk. Head coach Gregg Popovich and general manager R.C. Buford saw something in Kawhi that others had overlooked: his defensive instincts, his work ethic, and his potential to become a two-way player.

While Kawhi was initially shocked by the trade, it proved to be the best possible landing spot for the young forward. The Spurs, renowned for their player development and team-first culture, were the ideal environment for Kawhi to grow.

Early Career Struggles and Mentorship Under Gregg Popovich and Tim Duncan

Kawhi's first season with the Spurs in 2011-2012 was far from glamorous. The NBA lockout shortened the season, limiting opportunities for rookies to acclimate to the league. Additionally, Kawhi had to adjust to the Spurs' demanding system, which required precision, discipline, and a deep understanding of the game. For a rookie, this was no easy task.

In those early years, Kawhi struggled to find his place offensively, often deferring to the team's established stars like Tim Duncan, Tony Parker, and Manu Ginóbili. However, his defense and rebounding made an immediate impact. Kawhi's ability to guard multiple positions and disrupt opponents with his massive wingspan and quick hands earned him playing time and the trust of his coaches.

A critical part of Kawhi's growth during this time was the mentorship he received from head coach Gregg Popovich and veteran teammates, particularly Tim Duncan. Popovich challenged Kawhi to be more vocal, a difficult task for someone as naturally reserved as Kawhi. He also encouraged Kawhi to expand his game, pushing him to work on his shooting and offensive versatility.

Tim Duncan, meanwhile, became a quiet mentor for Kawhi. As one of the greatest power forwards in NBA history, Duncan exemplified professionalism, humility, and dedication to the team. Kawhi observed Duncan's work ethic and approach to the game, adopting many of the same principles in his development.

Transition From Role Player to Defensive Stalwart

Kawhi's transition from a role player to a defensive stalwart began in earnest during his second season. With increased playing time and more responsibility on defense, he quickly established himself as one of the league's premier wing defenders. Kawhi's defensive prowess was on full display during the Spurs' 2013 playoff run, where he was tasked with guarding some of the league's top scorers.

The defining moment of his early defensive dominance came during the 2013 NBA Finals against the Miami Heat. Although the Spurs ultimately lost the series in seven games, Kawhi's performance against LeBron

James was a revelation. He held his own against one of the game's greatest players, showing poise and determination that belied his age and experience.

Kawhi's work ethic during the offseason further propelled his growth. He worked tirelessly to improve his jump shot, studying film and tweaking his shooting mechanics. The results were evident as his offensive game began to complement his already elite defense.

By the end of his second season, Kawhi was no longer just a promising young player—he was an integral part of the Spurs' system. His ability to shut down opposing players and contribute on offense made him a rising star in the league. The foundation was set for what would become a remarkable career, built on the values of discipline, humility, and relentless self-improvement.

Kawhi Leonard's entry into the NBA was not without its struggles, but his journey during those early years with the San Antonio Spurs highlighted his resilience and capacity for growth. Under the guidance of one of the league's most respected organizations, Kawhi transitioned from an overlooked rookie to a cornerstone of the Spurs' future. His early years laid the groundwork for a career defined by excellence, a quiet determination, and an unwavering commitment to being the best.

CHAPTER 5: RISE TO STARDOM

Kawhi Leonard's rise to stardom was as remarkable as it was understated. During his tenure with the San Antonio Spurs, he developed into one of the most dominant two-way players in the league, earning accolades and recognition for his transformative performances. This chapter explores his breakout during the 2014 NBA Finals, his ascent to superstardom as a Finals MVP, and the challenges he faced, including injuries and adversity, during his time with the Spurs.

Breakout Performances in the 2014 NBA Finals

The 2014 NBA Finals marked a turning point in Kawhi Leonard's career. After falling to the Miami Heat in the previous year's Finals, the Spurs entered the rematch with a vengeance. While the team's seasoned core of Tim

Duncan, Tony Parker, and Manu Ginóbili led the way, it was Kawhi who became the series' unexpected hero.

Initially, Kawhi struggled to find his rhythm, scoring just nine points in Game 1. However, in Game 3, everything changed. Matched up against LeBron James, Kawhi delivered a stunning performance on both ends of the floor. His defensive intensity disrupted the Heat's offensive flow, while his offensive efficiency—scoring 29 points on 10-for-13 shooting—helped the Spurs secure a blowout win.

From that point onward, Kawhi's confidence soared. Throughout the series, he averaged 17.8 points, 6.4 rebounds, and 1.6 steals per game while shooting an incredible 61.2% from the field. His ability to guard LeBron James effectively, combined with his offensive contributions, was instrumental in the Spurs' dominant 4-1 series victory.

Winning the NBA Finals MVP and Becoming a League Superstar

Kawhi Leonard was named the NBA Finals MVP, becoming the youngest player to win the award since Magic Johnson. His breakout performance solidified his place among the league's elite, but true to his nature, Kawhi accepted the honor with quiet humility. "I'm just happy we won," he said during the trophy presentation, a statement that encapsulated his team-first mentality.

The Finals MVP award catapulted Kawhi into the national spotlight. Suddenly, he was no longer just a promising young player—he was a bona fide star with the potential to become the face of the Spurs. Analysts praised his ability to impact games on both ends of the floor, dubbing him one of the best two-way players in the league.

For Kawhi, the recognition was well-earned but never a distraction. He remained focused on his craft, working tirelessly during the offseason to refine his skills. His ability to stay grounded despite the accolades endeared him to fans and teammates alike, further establishing his reputation as a humble yet fierce competitor.

Challenges and Injuries During His Tenure with the Spurs

Despite his meteoric rise, Kawhi's time with the Spurs was not without its challenges. As his role on the team expanded, so too did the physical and mental demands placed on him. The wear and tear of an 82-game season, combined with the intensity of playoff basketball, began to take a toll on his body.

During the 2016-2017 season, Kawhi reached new heights, finishing third in MVP voting while averaging a career-high 25.5 points per game. However, injuries started to cast a shadow over his career. The most significant setback came during the 2017 Western Conference Finals against the Golden State Warriors. In Game 1, Kawhi suffered an ankle injury after landing on Zaza Pachulia's foot during a jump shot. The controversial play sidelined him for the remainder of the series, and the Spurs were swept.

The following season was marred by a mysterious quadriceps injury that limited Kawhi to just nine games. The injury strained his relationship with the Spurs organization, as conflicting reports about his rehabilitation created tension between Kawhi's camp and the team. While the Spurs' medical staff cleared him to play, Kawhi and his advisors opted for a more cautious approach, leading to a growing rift.

For a player as reserved as Kawhi, the public scrutiny surrounding his injury was especially challenging. Accusations of selfishness and speculation about his commitment to the team began to surface, further complicating the situation. Ultimately, the strained relationship led to Kawhi requesting a trade during the 2018 offseason, signaling the end of his time in San Antonio.

Kawhi Leonard's rise to stardom with the Spurs showcased his ability to thrive on the biggest stages and overcome adversity. His breakout in the 2014 NBA Finals and subsequent Finals MVP performance solidified his place among the NBA's elite, while the challenges he faced during his tenure demonstrated his resilience and determination. Though his time in San Antonio ended on a sour note, it was also where Kawhi established himself as one of the game's brightest stars and laid the foundation for the next chapter of his illustrious career.

CHAPTER 6: THE TORONTO RAPTORS ERA

Kawhi Leonard's tenure with the Toronto Raptors may have lasted only a single season, but its impact reverberated throughout the basketball world and cemented his legacy as one of the NBA's all-time greats. From the controversial trade that brought him to Canada to his heroics during the Raptors' historic 2018-19 season, Kawhi's time in Toronto was nothing short of legendary. This chapter explores the defining moments of his Raptors era, including the seismic trade, his transformative impact on the team and city, the unforgettable championship run, and "The Shot" that solidified his Finals MVP honors.

Controversial Trade to the Raptors

In the summer of 2018, Kawhi Leonard's relationship with the San Antonio Spurs had reached a breaking point.

Amid ongoing tension surrounding his quadriceps injury and its treatment, Kawhi requested a trade, sending shockwaves through the NBA. The Spurs, reluctant to deal their star to a Western Conference rival, found a trade partner in the Toronto Raptors, who were eager to shake up their roster after repeated playoff disappointments.

The trade was a gamble for both sides. The Raptors sent beloved franchise cornerstone DeMar DeRozan, along with Jakob Poeltl and a first-round pick, to San Antonio in exchange for Kawhi Leonard and Danny Green. For Toronto, it was a risky move: Kawhi was coming off an injury-riddled season and was set to become a free agent in 2019. Many doubted whether he would even consider staying in Toronto long-term.

For Kawhi, the move was bittersweet. Although it offered a fresh start, he was heading to an unfamiliar city with a team that had yet to prove itself as a championship contender. Despite initial skepticism, Kawhi approached the new chapter with his trademark professionalism and focus.

Impact on the Team and City of Toronto

From the moment Kawhi donned a Raptors jersey, his presence transformed the team. His leadership on the court, combined with Danny Green's veteran savvy, elevated the Raptors to a new level of competitiveness. Kawhi's impact extended beyond his stats; his calm demeanor and unrelenting work ethic set the tone for the entire roster.

The city of Toronto embraced Kawhi as a superstar and savior. Despite his reserved nature and reluctance to engage with the media, fans rallied behind him, coining phrases like "King of the North" to celebrate his dominance. Toronto's diverse and passionate fan base, already known as one of the most dedicated in the NBA, became electrified by the possibility of a championship.

Kawhi's presence also influenced the Raptors' culture. Under head coach Nick Nurse, the team embraced a defensive identity that mirrored Kawhi's tenacity and discipline. Players like Kyle Lowry, Pascal Siakam, and Fred VanVleet flourished alongside Kawhi, creating a cohesive and dynamic unit capable of taking on the league's best.

Historic 2018-19 Season and NBA Championship Win

The 2018-19 season was nothing short of magical for the Raptors. Kawhi played in 60 regular-season games as part of a carefully managed "load management" strategy designed to keep him healthy for the playoffs. Despite the limited appearances, Kawhi averaged 26.6 points, 7.3 rebounds, and 3.3 assists per game, reaffirming his status as one of the NBA's elite players.

The playoffs, however, were where Kawhi truly ascended to legendary status. After dispatching the Orlando Magic in the first round, the Raptors faced the Philadelphia 76ers in a grueling seven-game series.

"The Shot" Against the 76ers

Game 7 against the 76ers provided one of the most iconic moments in NBA history. With the score tied at 90 and just seconds remaining, Kawhi received an inbound pass, dribbled to the corner, and launched a contested fadeaway jumper over Joel Embiid. The ball bounced on the rim four times before finally dropping through the net as the buzzer sounded.

"The Shot" was more than just a game-winner—it was a defining moment for Kawhi's career and Raptors history. The image of Kawhi crouched on the baseline, watching the ball fall through the hoop, became an enduring symbol of his poise under pressure. The Raptors advanced to the Eastern Conference Finals, where they defeated the Milwaukee Bucks in six games to reach the NBA Finals.

Finals MVP Honors

In the NBA Finals, the Raptors faced the heavily favored Golden State Warriors, a dynasty led by Stephen Curry, Klay Thompson, and Draymond Green. Despite the Warriors' pedigree, Kawhi led Toronto to a stunning 4-2 series victory, averaging 28.5 points, 9.8 rebounds, and

4.2 assists per game. His two-way dominance neutralized the Warriors' firepower and anchored the Raptors' attack.

Kawhi was named Finals MVP for the second time in his career, becoming the first player in NBA history to win the award with teams from both conferences. His ability to rise to the occasion, particularly in high-pressure moments, solidified his legacy as one of the greatest playoff performers in NBA history.

Kawhi Leonard's lone season with the Toronto Raptors was nothing short of transformative. He not only brought the franchise its first NBA championship but also left an indelible mark on the team, the city, and the league. His heroics during the 2018-19 season, capped by "The Shot" and his Finals MVP performance, remain etched in basketball lore, a testament to his ability to thrive in the biggest moments.

CHAPTER 7: LA CLIPPERS JOURNEY

Kawhi Leonard's decision to join the Los Angeles Clippers in 2019 marked the beginning of a new chapter in his storied career. Returning to his hometown of Los Angeles, Kawhi sought to bring a championship to a franchise that had long been overshadowed by the success of its cross-town rivals, the Lakers. However, his time with the Clippers has been marked by lofty aspirations, leadership challenges, and significant setbacks, all of which have tested his resilience and resolve.

The decision to Join the Los Angeles Clippers

Following his historic championship run with the Toronto Raptors in the 2018-19 season, Kawhi became one of the most sought-after free agents in NBA history. While the Raptors hoped to retain him and other teams, including the Lakers, made their pitches, Kawhi ultimately chose the Clippers.

His decision was influenced by multiple factors. Returning to Southern California allowed him to play closer to home and his family. Additionally, the Clippers' front office, led by Steve Ballmer, Lawrence Frank, and Jerry West, presented Kawhi with a vision of building a championship team from the ground up—one that would revolve around his talents.

Another key factor in Kawhi's decision was the acquisition of Paul George. Kawhi reportedly pushed for the Clippers to trade for George, another Southern California native and All-NBA talent. The team obliged, sending a massive haul of draft picks and players to the Oklahoma City Thunder to pair the two stars. The move signaled the Clippers' commitment to winning and set the stage for a new era of high expectations.

Aspirations to Bring a Championship to His Hometown

For Kawhi, joining the Clippers was more than just a career decision—it was personal. Growing up in Riverside, California, Kawhi had always dreamed of bringing an NBA championship to his hometown. While the Lakers had long dominated the city's basketball scene, the Clippers represented an opportunity to build something unique and to carve out his legacy.

The expectations were immense. With Kawhi and Paul George leading the way, the Clippers were immediately thrust into championship contention. The team's roster featured a mix of experienced veterans like Lou Williams and Patrick Beverley, as well as promising young players.

Many analysts predicted that the Clippers would not only contend for a title but potentially end the Lakers' reign as the city's premier team.

Leadership Challenges and Playing Alongside Paul George

Kawhi's role as the centerpiece of the Clippers came with significant leadership responsibilities. While his quiet demeanor and lead-by-example approach had worked in previous stops, the Clippers' unique dynamics presented new challenges.

One of the key adjustments was building chemistry with Paul George. Though both players shared a similar mindset as two-way stars, finding a rhythm on the court took time. Injuries and lineup changes further complicated the process, making it difficult for the duo to establish consistency.

Leadership challenges also extended to the broader team dynamic. The Clippers' star-powered roster sometimes struggled with cohesion, as reports of locker room tension and disagreements over player roles emerged. As the team's leader, Kawhi faced the challenge of uniting a group with diverse personalities and expectations.

Reflections on Injuries, Setbacks, and Perseverance

Kawhi's time with the Clippers has been plagued by injuries, testing his resilience and ability to persevere. In the 2020 NBA Playoffs, the Clippers suffered a stunning collapse, losing a 3-1 lead to the Denver Nuggets in the Western Conference Semifinals. The loss was a major disappointment for a team expected to contend for a championship.

The following season, Kawhi's exceptional play led the Clippers to the Western Conference Finals for the first time in franchise history. However, an ACL injury during the 2021 playoffs derailed their championship hopes and sidelined Kawhi for the entire 2021-22 season. His absence was a significant blow to the team and raised questions about his long-term health.

Despite these setbacks, Kawhi's commitment to returning stronger has never wavered. His meticulous approach to recovery and dedication to his craft reflect the resilience that has defined his career. While injuries have limited his time on the court, Kawhi has continued to serve as a leader and motivator for his team, emphasizing the importance of perseverance in the face of adversity.

A Complex Legacy

Kawhi Leonard's journey with the LA Clippers is still being written, but it is already a story of ambition, challenges, and resilience. His decision to join the team was rooted in a desire to achieve greatness on his terms, and while injuries and setbacks have posed significant obstacles, Kawhi remains focused on his ultimate goal: delivering a championship to his hometown.

Whether or not Kawhi and the Clippers achieve this goal, his time with the team has solidified his status as one of the most determined and impactful players of his generation. Kawhi's journey serves as a reminder that greatness is not only measured by accolades but also by the ability to rise above challenges and stay true to one's vision.

CHAPTER 8: PERSONALITY AND OFF-COURT LIFE

Kawhi Leonard's life off the court is as intriguing as his accomplishments on it. Known for his famously private and introverted nature, Kawhi has managed to remain an enigma in a world where social media and constant public attention dominate the lives of most NBA stars. This chapter delves into Kawhi's personality, his interests outside basketball, and the unique ways in which the media and fans perceive him.

Kawhi's Famously Private and Introverted Nature

Kawhi Leonard has often been described as the "quiet superstar." Unlike many of his peers, Kawhi avoids the limelight and has little interest in promoting his brand through social media or interviews. This reserved nature has become one of his defining traits, making him stand out in a league filled with extroverted personalities.

For Kawhi, privacy isn't just a preference—it's a lifestyle. He rarely shares details about his personal life, and his interviews are often concise and focused on basketball. His reluctance to open up has led to a perception of him as mysterious, but those who know him well describe Kawhi as thoughtful, funny, and deeply loyal to those in his inner circle.

Kawhi's low profile extends to his approach to fame. While other athletes might embrace endorsements and public appearances, Kawhi keeps his focus on the game, prioritizing family and personal growth over public adoration. This commitment to staying grounded has endeared him to fans who admire his humility and work ethic.

Interests Outside Basketball: Family Life, Business Ventures, and Philanthropy

Off the court, Kawhi Leonard is a family man. He places tremendous value on his relationships, especially with his long-term partner, Kishele Shipley, and their children. Kawhi's family serves as a source of motivation and strength, grounding him amidst the pressures of professional sports. Despite his demanding schedule, he prioritizes spending time with his loved ones whenever possible.

Beyond family, Kawhi has ventured into business. In 2020, he collaborated with New Balance, his primary endorsement partner, to launch his signature basketball shoe line. His partnership with the brand has been a reflection of his individuality, aligning with their shared ethos of authenticity and dedication to craft. Kawhi has also been involved in community initiatives, supporting programs that promote education, youth development, and disaster relief.

One of his most notable philanthropic efforts occurred in 2019 when Kawhi partnered with the Los Angeles Clippers Foundation and Baby2Baby to donate one million backpacks to Southern California students. This gesture, rooted in his commitment to giving back to the community, highlighted his quiet but impactful approach to helping others.

The "Fun Guy" Meme and Media Portrayal

Despite his reserved personality, Kawhi Leonard has had his share of viral moments. During his introductory press conference with the Toronto Raptors, Kawhi's awkward yet endearing laugh while declaring, "I'm a fun guy," instantly became an internet sensation. The moment spawned countless memes and cemented his status as a cultural icon in an unexpected way.

The "Fun Guy" meme showcased a rare glimpse of Kawhi's humor, endearing him to fans who found joy in his unintentional comedic timing. It also reflected a broader theme in how the media portrays Kawhi—as a serious, enigmatic figure whose occasional moments of levity are celebrated precisely because they are so rare.

Kawhi's relationship with the media has always been complex. While some see his quiet nature as a lack of engagement, others appreciate his focus and refusal to conform to the expectations of celebrity culture. Kawhi remains steadfast in his belief that actions speak louder than words, letting his performance on the court define his legacy.

An Authentic Legacy

Kawhi Leonard's personality and off-court life provide a compelling contrast to his dominance in basketball. His commitment to privacy, dedication to his family, and understated sense of humor have made him a unique figure in the sports world. While the media and fans often speculate about the man behind the stoic exterior, those closest to Kawhi understand that his authenticity and humility are his greatest strengths.

In a world that often demands visibility and self-promotion, Kawhi Leonard has carved out a legacy built on substance over style. His ability to stay true to himself, both on and off the court, is a testament to the character and values that have guided him throughout his life.

CHAPTER 9: LEGACY AND IMPACT

Kawhi Leonard's legacy transcends statistics, championships, and accolades. His contributions to the game of basketball, his influence on younger players and fans, and the respect he has earned from coaches, teammates, and competitors have cemented his place among the sport's all-time greats. This chapter explores how Kawhi has shaped the game, inspired a new generation, and left an indelible mark on everyone who has crossed paths with him.

Contributions to the Game of Basketball

Kawhi Leonard's impact on basketball begins with his mastery of the two-way game. Few players in NBA history have combined elite offensive and defensive skills as seamlessly as Kawhi. His ability to guard multiple positions, disrupt opposing offenses, and make game-changing plays on defense earned him two NBA Defensive Player of the Year awards and solidified his reputation as one of the best defenders of his generation.

Offensively, Kawhi's evolution has been just as remarkable. From his early days as a defensive specialist with the San Antonio Spurs to becoming a dominant scoring force capable of carrying a team, his growth has been a testament to his tireless work ethic and commitment to improvement. He is known for his mid-range excellence, precise footwork, and ability to perform under pressure, particularly in playoff moments that define legacies.

Beyond his on-court achievements, Kawhi has contributed to a broader understanding of player load management. While controversial at times, his use of strategic rest has sparked conversations about the balance between athlete performance and longevity. Kawhi's approach has influenced how teams manage their star players, prioritizing long-term health over short-term gains.

Influence on Younger Players and Fans

Kawhi's story of perseverance, humility, and excellence has inspired countless young players and fans around the world. For aspiring athletes, Kawhi serves as a model of how hard work and discipline can elevate natural talent to extraordinary levels. His journey from an overlooked high school recruit to a two-time NBA Finals MVP exemplifies the value of determination and resilience.

Younger players also admire Kawhi's unique approach to the game. In an era dominated by social media and flashy personalities, Kawhi stands out for his quiet confidence and focus on substance over style. His preference for letting his performance speak for itself has resonated with those who value humility and professionalism.

Fans, particularly in Toronto and San Antonio, hold a special place in their hearts for Kawhi. In Toronto, his contributions to the Raptors' first NBA championship made him a beloved figure, while in San Antonio, he is remembered for his role in continuing the Spurs' legacy of excellence. Even in Los Angeles, where his journey with the Clippers continues, Kawhi's influence is seen in the franchise's pursuit of greatness.

Reflections from Coaches, Teammates, and Competitors

The people who have worked closest with Kawhi Leonard—his coaches, teammates, and competitors—speak of him with universal respect and admiration.

Gregg Popovich, Kawhi's former coach with the San Antonio Spurs, has often praised Kawhi's work ethic and willingness to learn. "He's one of the most coachable players I've ever had," Popovich once said. "He just goes about his business and doesn't need the spotlight."

Nick Nurse, who coached Kawhi during the Raptors' championship run, described him as the ultimate professional. "He never let the moment get too big. He kept the team steady with his calm demeanor and his incredible ability to perform under pressure."

Paul George, Kawhi's teammate with the Los Angeles Clippers, has spoken about Kawhi's leadership. "He doesn't have to say much because he leads by example. You see how hard he works, and it pushes everyone around him to be better."

Competitors have also shared their admiration for Kawhi's game. LeBron James, one of Kawhi's fiercest rivals, has called him "one of the toughest players to go up against," highlighting Kawhi's ability to excel on both ends of the court. Kevin Durant has similarly noted that Kawhi's defense and offensive efficiency make him "a nightmare to play against."

Kawhi Leonard's legacy is one of excellence, humility, and perseverance. He has reshaped expectations for what a superstar can be, proving that greatness doesn't require constant self-promotion or bravado. His ability to rise to the occasion in the biggest moments and his dedication to improving every facet of his game serves as a blueprint for success in basketball and beyond.

While Kawhi's career is far from over, his impact on the game is already undeniable. He will be remembered as one of the most complete players of his era, a two-time champion, a Finals MVP, and a role model for generations of athletes to come. His journey is a testament to the power of quiet determination and the enduring legacy of a man who let his actions speak louder than his words.

CONCLUSION

Kawhi Leonard's journey from a quiet, hardworking kid in Riverside, California, to a two-time NBA champion and Finals MVP is a story of perseverance, focus, and unrelenting dedication to excellence. Across each chapter of his life and career—whether it was his early days of discovery, his collegiate rise at San Diego State, or his triumphs and challenges in the NBA—Kawhi has proven that greatness is achieved not through words, but through action.

Summary of His Journey and Achievements

Kawhi's basketball journey is a testament to his ability to overcome adversity. From his humble beginnings, shaped by family values and personal loss, to his evolution into one of the game's most dominant two-way players, his path has been anything but ordinary.

His career is marked by defining moments that demonstrate his unwavering resolve:

His emergence as a defensive stalwart with the San Antonio Spurs, culminated in a 2014 NBA Finals MVP and championship victory.

His transformative single season with the Toronto Raptors, where he delivered the franchise's first NBA title and crafted unforgettable moments like "The Shot."

His ongoing quest to bring a championship to his hometown with the Los Angeles Clippers, despite facing injuries and setbacks along the way.

Through it all, Kawhi has compiled an impressive resume: multiple NBA championships, Finals MVPs, Defensive Player of the Year honors, and countless other accolades that solidify his place among the all-time greats.

Final Thoughts on His Lasting Legacy in Basketball and Sports Culture

Kawhi Leonard's legacy is multifaceted. On the court, he will be remembered as one of the most complete players the game has ever seen—a relentless defender, an efficient scorer, and a player who thrives in the game's biggest moments. Off the court, his humility and privacy have set him apart in an era dominated by social media and self-promotion. Kawhi has shown that you don't need to chase the spotlight to achieve greatness; the spotlight will find you if you stay true to your craft.

In the broader culture of sports, Kawhi represents the power of quiet determination. His story has inspired countless young athletes to focus on the fundamentals, trust their journey, and remain resilient in the face of challenges. He has proven that legacy is not just about individual accolades but also about the impact you leave on those who come after you.

As Kawhi Leonard's career continues, one thing is certain: his contributions to basketball and his influence on the next generation will endure for decades to come. Kawhi's journey is a reminder that greatness is not defined by how loudly you declare it but by the actions you take and the example you set. In the world of sports, few have embodied this truth as completely as Kawhi Leonard.

Made in the USA
Coppell, TX
16 February 2025